The Day It Rained Mashed Potato
and More Crazy-But-True Stories

D1143975

Before becoming a writer, Jonathan Clements had about two hundred different jobs — he has been a gravedigger, Admiralty chart-compiler, dustman, artist, actor, milkman, roadsweeper, poet, greengrocer, life-saver, photographer, advertising copywriter, footballer and singer. *The Day It Rained Mashed Potato* is his seventh book for children. He lives on Salisbury Plain in Wiltshire.

The Day It Rained Mashed Potato

and More Crazy-But-True Stories

compiled by Jonathan Clements

with drawings by Roger Smith

An Armada Original

The Day It Rained Mashed Potato and More Crazy-But-True Stories was first published in the U.K. in 1978 by
Fontana Paperbacks,
14 St. James's Place, London SW1A 1PF.

© Jonathan Clements 1978

Printed in Great Britain by
Love & Malcomson Ltd., Brighton Road,
Redhill, Surrey.

Contents

CHAPTER ONE

Modern Madness

We live in an age of technological tomfoolery. It's an age when, although mankind has conquered the mysteries of space-travel, we still have to queue for hours in traffic jams to travel a few miles on Earth. And the world seems to get crazier every day. Just glance at the daily newspaper and you learn of all sorts of weird things. For instance, you can actually *eat* the paper you're reading! We live in a crazy world all right—as is proved by the following true tales of people and pickled pigsfeet caught up in the peculiar pantomime we call Life Today.

Heavenly Hot-Pot

The town of King's Lynn, in Norfolk, was hit by a freak snow-storm in August, 1973. But on closer inspection the white flakes bore a striking resemblance to mashed potato. It turned out that they actually *were* mashed potato, in instant form, and the white flakes covered cars and houses—and even turned black cats white.

The cause of the potato-flake storm was a malfunctioning machine in a local factory. Instead of pouring a mashed potato mixture into little bags, the machine was discharging the substance into the air in great quantities. The instant potato then soared up into the clouds, all fifty tons of it, and, when shortly afterwards it rained, the flakes were distributed over a wide area.

Heavenly Clock

According to astrologers, if all the stars in the northern sky are visible, you can set your watch within fifteen minutes of the correct time, and without the use of a complicated chart. The Pole Star is considered to be the centre of a huge clock, and the pointer of the Dipper, the hour hand. The number 6 will be below the Pole Star and the number 12 above. Taking the time as indicated by the Dipper's pointers, you can add to that figure the number of months that have elapsed since the 1st of January to the nearest quarter-month. The resulting sum is doubled and subtracted from $16\frac{1}{4}$. If the result is more than $16\frac{1}{4}$, subtract it from $40\frac{1}{4}$. The answer is time in hours after noon. For instance: it is late September, and the pointers of the sky-clock correspond to the position of the hour hand at 7 o'clock. $8\frac{3}{4}$ months have elapsed since New Year's Day. This is added to 7, making it $15\frac{3}{4}$. Double this is $31\frac{1}{2}$. Subtracting this from $40\frac{1}{4}$ gives $8\frac{3}{4}$ or 8.45 p.m.

What's for Afters?

S.S. Cardiff, a merchantman laden with a twin cargo of timber and tapioca powder, was about to dock at Cardiff in South Wales in October, 1974, when the timber caught fire. The crew confined the fire to one hold by wetting down the wood, but the fire brigade on shore drenched the ship with thousands of gallons of water. This seeped into the holds where the tapioca was stored, turning the powder into a watery gruel which was then cooked by the heat from the blazing timber. The ever-swelling ocean of syrupy tapioca pudding threatened to burst the ship's hull and a fleet of lorries had to relieve the *Cardiff* of about seven million gallons of cooked tapioca.

9

Clean-Cut Kids

The population of Great Britain is the cleanest of any nation in Europe, according to a study by the Swiss Union of Soap and Detergent Manufacturers. In 1975, the average consumption of soap throughout the British Isles was 3lb 2oz per person. Switzerland was runner-up with 2lb 11oz, followed by Germany with 2lb 6oz, Sweden with 2lb 2oz, France with 1lb 10oz, and the Netherlands with 1lb 5oz. Lowest was Italy, with a consumption of soap of only 7oz per person.

Health Hazards

The smoking hazard that Elizabeth Dickenson of Clapham, London, encountered in 1976 goes far beyond the health warning printed on cigarette packets. Mrs Dickenson took a gun from a drawer and went to investigate during the night when she thought she heard a burglar prowling about in her house. Finding nothing, she put the gun on the bedside table and went back to sleep. According to Mrs Dickenson, the next morning she awoke, took a cigarette from a packet, reached to the bedside table for the gun-shaped table lighter she keeps there—and shot herself in the right hand.

It's a Pig's Life

The Japanese are raising pigs to be astronauts. According to reports, the Japan Livestock Research Institute has developed an unusually small breed of swine to be used in space flights in the 1980s by the National Aeronautics and Space Administration. Meanwhile, earthbound porkers will reap whatever benefits result from a five-year study now in operation at the Agricultural Research Council in Cambridgeshire on what makes pigs bored, what makes them happy, and how to help them sleep well. The test subjects are being housed in air-conditioned, sound-proofed, luxurious underground bunkers during the study.

Railway Runaways

One day in 1886, a driverless railway engine ran from Pet-worth to Horsham in Surrey. Before being stopped by a cleaner trapped on board, the engine had travelled over seventeen miles and had four sets of level-crossing gates wrapped around its buffers. By a strange twist of coincidence, in 1972, some eighty-six years later, a driverless electric train ran eight miles between Caterham and Norwood in Surrey before being stopped. This train also had four sets of level-crossing gates wrapped around its buffers.

Bad for Bookworms

You've heard of Athlete's Foot and Housemaid's Knee—but would you believe there's such an ailment as Historian's Lung? Well, there is: a bronchial affliction marked by shortness of breath, coughing and wheezing, and general fatigue, brought on by excessive exposure to old books. In a report in *Science Digest*, Wilfred Spencer, a British librarian, described his own symptoms. "I spent eight hours a week moving old books around and arranging them. I was right in the middle of a pretty horrific concentration of mouldy documents. I became increasingly breathless, and my health became progressively worse." He recalled that the pages of some of the dustier tomes he had been handling were festooned with tiny fungi—virus-infected fungi, it turned out. Now warnings have been issued to the British Libraries' Association and the Society of Archivists.

Paddle-Post

In 1968, when the crew of a German tanker named *Hong Kong* learned that they would be steaming past Honolulu without stopping, they were furious, for they had been at sea for a month, and wanted to post their letters. There were some mutterings about a mutiny, but the resourceful captain came up with an ingenious method of mailing their letters. All the mail was packed into a large empty oil-drum, and tossed overboard. Several hours later the drum was spotted by the crew of a British patrol boat, who picked up the mysterious drum and opened it. Inside the drum they found, besides the letters, fifty pounds in cash, ten cartons of cigarettes and a crate of whisky to cover the postage and handling. The letters were in the mail that very afternoon.

Fatal Fire

On a May morning in 1921, A. V. Bonham, of Haywards Heath, Sussex, saw smoke. He was startled to learn that it was his own house on fire. Apparently, Bonham's eleven year-old son had used paraffin to start a bonfire, and an explosion that followed had set the house aflame.

With the aid of neighbours, Bonham removed most of his household goods, but forgot about his loaded revolver which lay in a bureau drawer. As Bonham stood sadly watching the hungry flames, a shot rang out. At the same instant Bonham cried out, "I am shot!" and, clutching his chest, he staggered a few steps and then fell dead. The heat had exploded Bonham's own gun, and the bullet had found his heart.

Prominent
Equatorial
Bulge ──→

Now He Tells Us

Word comes from Russian geophysicist, Dr Gaposchkin, that Mount Everest is not the world's highest mountain. What is, then? Well, it's Mount Chimborazo, in the Ecuadorian Andes.

Some explanation is in order: Dr Gaposchkin compared the height of the two peaks by measuring from *the Earth's centre* rather than from sea-level. The Earth, he points out, has a prominent equatorial bulge, and Chimborazo is situated right on top of that bulge, whereas Everest is located on a relatively flat part of the globe. As a result, Mount Everest's height, measured from the earth's centre, is 7,068 feet shorter than Mount Chimborazo (20,946,233 feet from the centre).

Hurry Up and Read Your Dinner!

Your morning newspaper is chock-full of cellulose, which is rich in carbohydrates. While carbohydrates in excess are not very good food value, Dr Steinkraus of the Swiss Agricultural Experimental Station in Geneva has pointed out that 1,000lbs of these carbohydrates, if fermented properly, can be turned into 12,000lbs of body-building protein. Properly-processed newsprint, he says, will be of great value as the world's food supplies dwindle over the centuries. Though somehow it sounds a little unappetising to draw your chair up to the table, put on your napkin and tuck into a big bundle of last week's Daily Mirrors ...

Stroke of Genius

In 1973, the Australian Army Material Command held a "Name - The - New - Headquarters - Building - And - Win - $100" competition. The AAMC's Competition sifted through some five thousand entries, a task that took them over a fortnight. And the winner? They finally settled on a name submitted by a certain Frank Sikorski. The name—wait for it—"The AAMC Building."

Creepy Cupboard

Is the high cost of dying getting you down? Then buy now and die later, says the Rocky Mountain Casket Company of Whitefish, Montreal, Canada. In 1976, the company's sturdy pine coffins were priced at only £80 each, prompting the advertising agency for the firm to urge potential customers to buy while prices were low. "The coffin can be used as a wine-rack or a small linen cupboard," proclaimed the advertisement, "until the buyer's time has come..."

Peculiar Punishments

In 1973, a Manchester magistrate sentenced a pickpocket to three months in jail for stealing £5 from a woman's handbag. Noting the defendant's record of twenty-five previous convictions, the magistrate also ordered the man to wear enormous 2lb fur gloves whenever he appeared in public for the next two years. However, the pickpocket, after serving his three months, disappeared.

Across the ocean, Pierre Morganti, the mayor of Olistro on the island of Corsica, announced in the summer of 1976 that anybody caught sunbathing in the nude on the beach there would be painted blue. Seven people were punished thus. Also in Corsica, in nearby Linguizetta, the town council, adopting the example of Lady Godiva, punishes minor offenders by making them ride naked through the streets on a donkey.

Wise Guys

Intelligence experts at Melbourne University, Australia, have determined that both John Stuart Mill (who could read and write Ancient Greek at the age of four) and Wolfgang von Goethe had I.Q.'s in the vicinity of 210. (An average person's I.Q. is 100—a figure of 150 is considered genius level.) Voltaire and Newton would probably have scored a respectable 190, Da Vinci 180, Shakespeare 175, Descartes 170, Galileo 160, and Napoleon 140. As for the living: a South Korean man named Kim Ung-Yong has chalked up a mammoth 205. By the time he was four years old, Ung-Yong could speak seven languages; and by the time he was seven, he could solve the most intricate problems in integral calculus. Just the kind of kid you would like to have sitting behind you at school to crib from!

Love's Stormy Path

Whilst stranded on a five-foot long raft for over a week in the storm-tossed Pacific Ocean with no water and nothing to eat except the raw meat of seagulls, Anthony Pike, a Singapore schooner captain, and Jennifer Fairfax-Ross, a fashion model from Sydney, Australia, fell in love and became engaged. They were rescued near Tahiti on June 23rd, 1975, and married on dry land a fortnight later.

No Votes As Yet

A rather strange nomination for the Presidency of the United States in 1975 was a certain Emil Matalik. When he announced that he was running for the office, he told reporters, "What I'm really interested in is being president of the world. The problems around the world are building up to an explosive point. As I see it, the only real solution is a world president—me."

Among the big problems, said Matalik, was "an overwhelming excess of animals and trees. Especially trees." Under the Matalik administration, each family would be permitted a maximum of one child, one dog and one tree. Matalik also said that his small pig-farm in Bennet, Wisconsin, would be the world capital just as soon as he got elected.

WORLD FAMILY UNIT. CIRCA. 1975

IN BRITAIN THERE IS A LONG TRADITION
OF ABSURD STUPIDITY

CHAPTER TWO

Those Lovable British Eccentrics!

The most extraordinary things happen in Britain, probably because it's inhabited by such a weird bunch of people. True, people abroad also act oddly (as you'll find out in another chapter), but in Britain there's a particularly long tradition of absurd stupidity. In what other country would you find a man committing suicide and leaving behind a note proving he was his own grandfather? Or where else would you come across the case of the female saint who sprouted a beard and moustache on her wedding night? Or the nut who built an aircraft carrier out of ice . . . ? To find out about these curious stories, and many others, why not lock yourself in a padded cell and read the whole chapter?

Hat Trick

When James Heatherington invented and wore the very first top hat in London, on January 5th, 1797, women fainted and young children screamed with alarm. So great was the commotion brought about by Heatherington's revolutionary headgear that he found himself summoned to appear before the Lord Mayor. He was bound over to keep the peace for the sum of £50, having been adjudged guilty of "appearing on a public highway wearing upon his head a tall structure having a shiny lustre and calculated to terrify people, frighten horses and disturb the balance of society".

Happy Dreams

Like many Victorians, the novelist Charles Dickens ensured himself of a good night's sleep by keeping the head of his bed aligned precisely with the North Pole, so that the earth's magnetic force would pass longitudinally through his body. Using similar logic, Islamic worshippers point their beds towards Mecca. Benjamin Disraeli was an insomniac and a believer in the occult. He was never able to fall asleep at night unless the four legs of his bed were planted in dishes filled with salt, to keep devilish spirits from attacking him.

The Lady Was a Tramp

In 1817, at the Assembly Rooms in Brighton, Lady Lutrell openly scolded the Prince Regent for dancing with Lady Laude, a vulgar, loud-mouthed, yet highly popular socialite. Yet Lady Lutrell herself was thrown into Newgate Prison for debts amounting to £50,000 just two years after this. She gained her freedom by marrying the prison barber, thus saddling him with her debts. Then Lady Lutrell fled to Augsberg in Germany, where she was arrested for picking pockets. Found guilty of the charge, she was sentenced to six months sweeping the streets, chained to a wheelbarrow. Eventually she was murdered one night for the contents of her purse, which contained the equivalent of about twenty pence.

Limp-along Lord

The Marquis of Anglesey had his leg amputated after an injury in the Battle of Waterloo. The leg was buried with full military honours in a nearby garden, with the Marquis proudly looking on. A hundred years later, the occupant of the cottage was still showing the grave as a tourist attraction, charging a halfpenny a look.

Calculator without Batteries

Jebediah Buxton, "the illiterate calculator" as he was known during his life, took a month to work out, without the aid of pen and paper, that a cubical mile could contain 586,040,972,673,025,000 human hairs—give or take a few. Having produced this highly valuable information, he then multiplied a farthing 140 times with itself. After three months of mental strife he arrived at the figure of £727,958, 238,096,074,979,868,531,654,993,638,851,106, 2 shillings and 8 pence.

Then some bigmouth happened to ask Jebediah if he'd care to multiply this sum by itself. It took him two and a half months to work out the result: £527,015,363,459,557, 385,673,733,542,638,951,744,808,079,307,524,906,381,389, 500,251,634,423,235.

Mr Big

Honest Jack Fuller, a politician in the eighteenth century, was known by nearly everybody as the Hippopotamus, because of his vast size. He was always ready to support the underdog—for instance, he gave the famous artist J. M. W. Turner food and shelter in his early days. Jack Fuller's appetite was prodigious; at a single sitting he could devour a whole hog's head, several pounds of beef, chicken, etc., and still have room for a whole five-pound chocolate pudding, a gallon of ale and a pint of claret. Fuller is buried in a fifteen-foot high pyramid in Brightling churchyard, Sussex —he is reputed to be at rest inside it sitting at a table with a bottle of claret before him and an eleven-course meal.

Dubious Dentistry

Martin Van Butchell, "Tooth-Drawer and Corn-Curer", travelled around the streets of London in the middle of the eighteenth century. Somewhat eccentric by nature, Butchell rode on a small pony painted with bright red spots ("so people can see me coming"), with a small blind let down over its eyes ("to prevent the stupid animal from panicking"). His charges, though, were reasonable: twopence halfpenny for extracting a tooth, and one penny for curing a corn. He would also perform the service of plucking chickens, charging a penny halfpenny a dozen. Butchell always carried with him a large bone—usually the thigh-bone of a horse—to protect himself against the thieves and rogues of London.

Earthshaking Hoaxes

In 1790, London suffered from a rash of false earthquake scares. The hoaxes were eventually traced to a crazy guardsman, Myer Weld, who issued pamphlets and ran around the streets shouting the bad news. On one occasion, over fifty thousand scared people flocked to empty spaces, including Hampstead Heath, to sleep out. Eventually, the insane guardsman was caught and sent to prison for life. The only people to gain from his peculiar notions were the London spivs, who made a fortune selling "anti-earthquake" pills.

Overdue Volumes

It took twenty-five removal men nearly four days to carry away all the books found in Phillip Grossman's five-roomed house in Fulham in 1968. Over 17,000 volumes—roughly eight lorry-loads—were piled from floor to ceiling in every room, also overflowing the sinks and the bath. This extraordinary library was discovered when firemen entered Grossman's house one day after receiving a report that there was smoke coming from there. Then they stumbled upon the books—all of them stolen from the London Library.

When Grossman, a fifty-seven-year-old labourer, was asked why he had stolen so many books, he replied, "I like to read." When it was revealed that he didn't even have a valid card for the London Library, everybody wondered how on earth he managed to get all those volumes out of the exclusive library. "Simple," said Grossman. "In very large quantities, over a period of years."

Cold-shouldered Ideas Department

Probably the craziest naval idea of all time was dreamed up in 1941 by a scientist named Lionel Pike. He was struck with the scheme to build an aircraft carrier out of ice. Code-named Habbakuk, the project was to construct a floating aerodrome two thousand feet long, three hundred feet wide and two hundred feet deep, out of two million tons of ice. This "ship" was to be covered in an insulating "skin" and kept permanently frozen. Work on this weird and wonderful project actually began in 1942, but the plan was scrapped after six months because of a small, almost insignificant detail. The aerodrome would keep sinking.

Whacky Worms

A somewhat drastic cure for tapeworms was invented by Dr Alpheus Meyers, of Sheffield, Yorkshire, in 1877. His patent "Tapeworm Trap" was a small metal cylinder, tied to a string and baited with food, which the patient swallowed after fasting long enough to work up the worm's appetite. Naturally, the tapeworm would poke its head into one end of the cylinder, where it would be caught by a metal spring strong enough to hold it tight, but not so strong that it would decapitate it. With the quarry thus trapped, the attending physicians would grasp the end of the string hanging from the patient's mouth and haul up the trap, parasite and all. A good idea—but after several people had choked to death using the contraption, it was suggested to Dr Meyers that perhaps his true vocation really lay in the invention of angling equipment.

Potty Peer

William John Cavendish Bentinck Scott, the 5th Duke of Cavendish, who lived in the nineteenth century, must have been the shyest person who ever lived. For a short while he occupied his inherited seat in the House of Lords, but he soon found he was too timid to take part in the debates. So at twenty he retired to his estate and withdrew further and further into himself. The Duke eventually shut himself off in one corner of his home, Welbeck Abbey. He refused to receive visitors, and he wouldn't even see his own servants. All communications with him were passed through a message-box outside his door. Then the Duke had a tunnel dug from Welbeck Abbey to the town of Worksop, one and a half miles away. Later, he had additional tunnels dug to his greenhouse and other outbuildings, eliminating any encounters with anybody during short walks. He lived in this way for another fifty years, dying, a virtual recluse, at the age of seventy.

35

Mr Muscle-man

Joseph Clark, a "Posture-Maker" as he called himself, lived in Pall Mall, London, around 1890. He could give himself a hump, a dislocated hip, or chronic knock-knees at will. His favourite practical joke involved going to a tailor to be measured for a new suit. Clark would develop an instant hump, then dislocate a shoulder, thereafter becoming completely normal. After the measurements had been taken, he would effect knock-knees and a dislocated hip—driving the poor baffled tailor to distraction.

Hired Hermits

The eighteenth century Gloucester eccentric, Charles Hamilton, apparently considered it a mark of esteem to have a real live hermit living in his garden. He offered handsome wages for the service, including a salary of £700 a year (equivalent to £7,000 today), and such valuable perks as a hair-shirt, an hour-glass, a rough sacking bed, and a Bible. In return, the hired hermit was expected to live in an artificial cave, not speak, and leave hair, nails and beard untrimmed. The one hermit Hamilton was able to lure into the position nearly went mad with boredom after six weeks, however, and ran away. A fellow-countryman of Hamilton's in Gloucester, though, had better luck, maintaining a hermit in a cave for nearly four years, but only on condition that the hermit be supplied with books, a bath-tub and a steam organ.

GENUINE HERMIT

Saints Alive!

St Wilgefortis was one of nine sisters born to an infidel king of Portugal. At an early age, Wilgefortis was converted to Christianity and took a vow of chastity, in spite of which her father betrothed her to the King of Sicily. The young girl prayed fervently for deliverance from the clutches of the Sicilian, and miraculously, on the day of her wedding, she sprouted a full black beard and moustache. Her fiancé lost interest. Her father, in a mad rage, had her crucified. St Wilgefortis is traditionally invoked in the prayers of maidens who wish to be rid of unwanted boyfriends. In Britain, she is known as "St Uncumber", prayed to by women who wish to unencumber themselves of husbands they do not love.

Baby-face

A strange anomaly of an aged youth attracted great attention during the last century. He was William Waddle, born in Staffordshire in 1829. He reached maturity by the age of one, could speak fluently by the age of two, and grew whiskers at the age of four. He died suddenly in a faint when he was only seven years old.

Waddle was of small stature and proportions, with imperfectly developed collar-bones, lower jaw, and membranes of the skull. His face was wizened, hair and whiskers snow-white, skin very shrivelled, hands and muscles knotted with conspicuous veins and tendons, voice high and piping, with the gait and standing posture of an extremely old man.

Who Was Who?

Edwin Wakeman, of Manchester, committed suicide in 1927, leaving behind him the following note:

"I married a widow with a grown daughter. My father fell in love with my step-daughter and married her—thus becoming my son-in-law. My step-daughter became my step-mother because she was my father's wife. My wife gave birth to a son, who was, of course, my father's brother-in-law, and also my uncle, for he was the brother of my step-mother. My father's wife became the mother of a son, who was, of course, my brother, and also my grandchild, for he was the son of my step-daughter. Accordingly, my wife was my grandmother, because she was my step-mother's mother. I was my wife's husband and grandchild at the same time. And, as the husband of a person's grandmother is his grandfather, I am *my own grandfather!*"

Small wonder the confused Mr Wakeman did himself in.

Naughty Vicar

The people of the village of Holyrood Ampney, in Gloucestershire, petitioned the House of Commons in 1855 to have their vicar excommunicated. The parson in question had the somewhat ill-fitting name of Benedict Grace. For in their petition, the villagers alleged that the Rev. Grace was: "a most unholy type of man. He is much given to drunkenness, shouting, and chasing young girls about the parish. Furthermore, the parson is uncivil, ignorant, uncharitable, lewd, cruel, and uses filthy un-Christian language..." The petition was successful, for the Rev. Benedict Grace disappeared shortly afterwards.

Bless You!

Margaret Thompson, a wealthy London socialite of the eighteenth century, had a passionate fondness for sneezing. When she died in 1776, her will directed that she should be buried in a coffin packed with snuff. She named the six most prodigious snuff-takers in London to be her pall-bearers, and they were instructed to wear snuff-coloured suits and beaver hats as they carried her remains to the cemetery. Six maidens preceded the cortege, inserting snuff into their own nostrils, distributing quantities of fine Scottish snuff to onlookers every twenty yards, and scattering snuff to the four winds like rose petals. The minister, for his services, and continued prayers, was bequeathed one pound of best snuff.

Dead Letter Day

David Spencer received an anonymous letter daily for twenty-five years, from the period 1908 till 1933. He was the owner of a greengrocer's shop in Guildford, Surrey, and after receiving the letter for a few years he grew tired of it, so he tried to get the Post Office to refrain from delivering his mail altogether. But in vain; the letters kept coming. Then suddenly in 1933 the letters ceased; it seemed that the tireless letter-writer had died at last.

Curiously enough, the contents of the letter was always the same, and quite innocent. They merely stated: "A stitch in time saves nine. A well-wisher."

Galloping Major

Major George Hanger, friend of the Prince Regent, once rode his horse up the stairs and into the attic of the house belonging to the fastidious Mrs Fitzherbert in Brighton. It needed eleven men, a crane and pulley and a blacksmith to get it down again. The Prince Regent was not amused. On another occasion, the madcap major harnessed a bull weighing four and a half tons and rode it up and down the Promenade at Brighton, much to the consternation of passers-by, many of whom fled into the sea.

CHAPTER THREE

Animal Antics

Would *you* paint your pet poodle pink? Did you know that worms can be university graduates? What would you do if you met a drunken elephant? Why are you being asked all these stupid questions? Do you think you'll get a prize if you get the answers right? Well, you won't. But what you will get is the satisfaction of knowing that you possess an inquisitive mind, and a thirst for knowledge. But no prizes. Now don't sulk and hide your head up the chimney—there are big treats in store. You're going to learn all sorts of odd things about the animal kingdom, including the strange subjects mentioned above. That is, if you manage to read this chapter before your dog eats it.

Chicken Drill

A public park in Melbourne, Australia, abounded with stop signs and other conventional traffic control devices, but many accidents still occurred—until City Park Superintendent Bob Walters hired eighty-six chickens as traffic-directors. Now the park is completely safe.

The chickens, of course, do nothing but strut about at the park's entrance, blithely oblivious to entering and exiting cars. But their very presence has helped reduce accidents—without the expense of hiring policemen. "The traffic moves with caution now," Walters explains. "Only occasionally does a mad driver charge through the flock." In the poultry patrol's first year of service, in 1975, only eight chickens were killed in the line of duty—a reasonable price to pay for traffic safety.

Traffic Director

And Elephants Are Pink . . .

Body-painting has long been an important ritual among the peasants of Iraq, but the bodies painted are those of farm animals, not the peasants themselves. Every spring, as the cycle of nature begins anew, the farmers get out their paints and brushes to appease the gods and fend off hostile spirits by painting their animals in a variety of colour schemes dictated by ancient fashion: green for the chickens, blue for the newly-hatched chicks; purple for the faces of the calves; red for the udders of the cows. Bulls are painted a brilliant pillar-box red, and horses a particularly sparkling silver.

Piggy Bank

Threadneedle Street, home of the Bank of England, was once called Pig Street, because of the pigs from the nearby hospital of St Anthony which roamed the streets and were fed by passers-by. In 1688, a man named Elia Foster was killed by a litter of pigs as he wended his way home through Pig Street. Thereafter the pigs were locked up, an' the name was changed in 1701 to Threadneedle Street because of all the seamstresses who worked there.

Hark! An Ant Hiccuping

Every year the British Wildlife Recording Society holds a competition to select the finest natural soundtracks in a variety of categories. For example, in 1972, Ray Goodwin of Gloucestershire won the coveted award for "Most Unusual Entry" with his tape of "A Roman Snail Chewing a Lettuce Leaf". This was highly amplified, sounding, as one reporter put it, "like a series of booming, crunching, ear-shattering noises lasting about two minutes." Among other Goodwin recordings that have won prizes are recordings of "A Dung Beetle at Play", and "A Pair of Butterflies Fighting". The winner of the Mammal division in 1974 was Arthur Acland, a seventy-year-old retired underwear salesman from Kent, with his irresistible entry: "A Humorous Recording of a Hedgehog Barking to Warn Off Other Spiny Members of his Tribe as He Sips a Bowl of Milk".

Animals Attack!

During the Battle of Rancagua in October, 1814, the Chilean patriot Bernado O'Higgins commanded a badly outnumbered army. The revolutionaries were surrounded by Spanish troops and were running low on ammunition. O'Higgins himself was wounded. There seemed to be no hope of fighting their way out of a desperate situation.

Then O'Higgins ordered his men to gather up every animal in the village—dogs, horses, cows, sheep, even ducks and chickens. With their remaining ammunition, the troops scared the animals into a frantic stampede. Mooing, barking, braying, the motley menagerie charged towards the enemy lines, scattering the terrified Spaniards in all directions. O'Higgins and his men took advantage of the confusion to ride through the breach and escape to freedom.

Boozing Birds

In Hawkshead, Lancashire, there is a well-known pub called "The Drunken Duck". Its unusual name derives from an incident that occurred there in 1788. One summer's day, beer seeped from the pub's cellar into the ducks' feed trough. The landlady found the ducks apparently dead, and she started plucking them and preparing them for the oven. Suddenly, the ducks started sobering up. The somewhat eccentric landlady made amends by knitting small garments for the ducks to wear, then returned them to their roost.

No Kidding

There is a rather strange breed of goats that lives only in a small area on the outskirts of Madrid, Spain. These are perhaps the most cowardly of all animals. Whenever they are startled by thunder, a tractor starting up, or even the clatter of a feed-bucket, the goats collapse in a dead faint. From a distance, it seems that they have died, but on closer examination one finds that the animals have lapsed into a rigid catatonic state. Moments later, the goats recover their senses and return to their grazing, apparently none the worse for their experience. Veterinary surgeons say the ailment is akin to *myotonia-congenita*, a disorder that causes involuntary nervous spasms in human beings. Señor Manello Velasquez of Madrid is one farmer who still raises the swooning goats. "They aren't good for anything," he says, "but they're pretty funny."

51

Besotted Beasts

Drunken elephants are quite a big problem in South Africa's Kruger National Park. It seems that they are particularly fond of the sweet fruits of the marula tree, which thrives within the park's boundaries. After a feast of marula fruit an elephant becomes terrifically thirsty and wanders off to the nearest stream to fill up on gallons of water. Intestinal fermentation then converts the fruit sugars to alcohol and leaves the giant animal thoroughly drunk. You can hear a drunken elephant from miles away; it trumpets wildly like a highly-amplified pop-group. Furthermore, a tipsy elephant loses all its inhibitions; it stampedes, squashing other animals, staggers about, and finally collapses in a stupor. Park officials are concerned about the property and livestock damage the animals cause on their drunken binges—but as yet there has been no suggestion that breathalyser tests are taken on the elephants.

Protected Species

America has some strange laws to protect its wildlife and its tamelife. For instance, it is illegal to "mistreat or otherwise hurt the feelings" of oysters in Baltimore, Maryland. And "fish-lassooing" is prohibited in Knoxville, Tennessee. In Arizona, kicking a mule (however stubborn) is a punishable offence. So is "deliberately worrying or chasing" squirrels in Topeka, Kansas. And in California, you are breaking the law if you pluck the feathers from a live goose.

A vegetarian postscript: vegetables have feelings too, you know. Since 1972, the Society for the Prevention of Cruelty to Mushrooms of Michigan, has zealously guarded the best interests of mushrooms. Anybody plucking and eating mushrooms is liable to a fine or a telling-off by the Society's three thousand members.

Rats in the Belfry

Dr K. N. Udupa, director of the Medical Institute of Benares Hindu University, India, trained six field rats to assume the yoga position of "Sirasana"—that is, standing on their heads—for up to three hours a day. Dr Udupa wired the rodents' heads to a battery of monitoring devices, including electro-cardiogram machines. He has discovered that, after first jolting the rats with electric shocks to make them tense, an hour of "Sirasana" calmed them down and returned their nerves to normal.

Uplift for Cows

Probably the most unusual bras in the world are made for cows. The Franksville Speciality Company of Johannesburg, South Africa, manufactures them and claims they're big sellers at approximately £22 a set. Useful rather than beautiful, the bras keep the cows from tripping over their own udders. All sizes are available up to 108 inches.

To Bee or Not To Bee

In 1955, a geneticist named Warrick Kerr imported seventy lethal African bees to his laboratory in Sao Paolo, Brazil. His aim was to study their breeding habits and learn how they could be safely crossbred with local bees to boost the Brazilian honey crop. However, Professor Kerr's bees had crossbreeding plans of their own. Twenty-six of them escaped from his lab in 1957, and within a few months there were several million offspring, each one every bit as deadly as its parents.

Drifting northward at a rate of two hundred miles a year, the deadly bees to date have passed through Bolivia, Paraguay, Peru and Venezuela, swarming down on humans and cattle alike without the slightest provocation. Since the first recorded fatality in 1964, the bees have disrupted weddings, garden parties, funeral processions and other outdoor events, claiming approxixmately a hundred and fifty victims, and millions of nasty bites. The experts are puzzled as to what to do—apart from arming everyone with a heavy bee-veil.

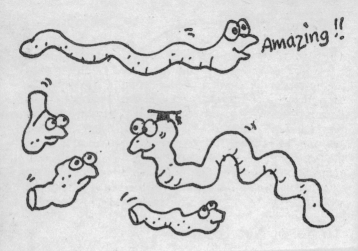

Worms That Turn

Probably the best-educated worms in captivity live in the laboratory of Dr James V. McConnel of the University of Ontario, Canada. With infinite patience, Dr McConnel taught planarians—the common worms found in streams and ponds—to crawl through a series of complex mazes. Then ruthlessly he cut his educated worms in half. As worms have the curious habit of doing, the head section grew a new tail and the tail section grew a new head. Both regenerated worms retained the maze-running skills of the original undivided specimen.

Next, McConnel took some trained worms, diced them into tiny morsels, and fed them to uneducated worms. Placed in the same maze that the "victims" had learned to run, the cannibal worms exhibited an uncanny sense of direction. Apparently, by devouring the trained worms they had also ingested their memories and maze-running abilities.

Gruesome Guards

The Sterling Works, a San Francisco jewellery shop, rents a five-year-old tarantula spider for £10 a month to guard their premises. The spider is displayed in the window of the shop, along with a bold sign that announces "Caution—This Area is Patrolled by a Poisonous Spider!" Since the Sterling Works installed the spider to guard their shop four years ago, they've had only one robber, as opposed to a dozen the year before. On the same subject, a Canadian gun-and-ammunition shop called The Bullet Hole warns away mischief-makers with a hundredweight lion named Beau, who stalks the building at night, emitting fearsome growls.

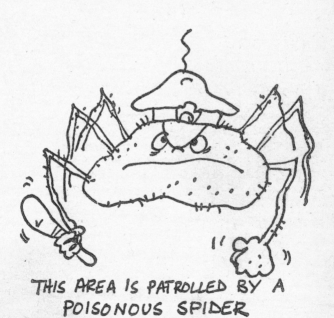

THIS AREA IS PATROLLED BY A POISONOUS SPIDER

Elephant Country

In May, 1910, an elephant named Charlie escaped from a circus at the Crystal Palace and rampaged loose all around Penge and Beckenham in South London. The worst damage he did, though, was treading on a man's foot, and demolishing scores of garden hedges and sheds. The circus people tried to trap him with poisoned buns, but he wouldn't be tempted. Eventually, after over a week of freedom, Charlie had to be shot on nearby Hayes Common.

CHAPTER FOUR

Foreign Freaks

There are strange games being played in foreign quarters. German nuns are biting each other, Chinamen are being born with transparent skin, and worse still, Danish astronomers are losing their noses in duels! In this stirring chapter you will learn of mad moments in places as far apart as Poland and Peru—Africa and Australia.

Stand Easy

At this very moment there are men standing by the River Nile near Kali-Ghat in India. That's all they ever do—just stand there.

Among the group of hundreds witnessed by a recent traveller, there were some men who had been standing there for over twenty years without once having sat or lain down. They seemed to be prepared to stand there for the rest of their lives. Their bodies and faces were smeared a dirty, sickly white, leaving two black spots for their eyes. They had forced two poles into the sand from which they were suspended on arm-rests. Nobody knows exactly why the men are standing there—least of all the men themselves.

Just Moving House

Henry Ford, famous pioneer of the motor car, was so fond of Rose Cottage at Chedsworth in the Cotswolds that he decided to take it home to America with him. Ford had the cottage dismantled, all the pieces numbered, and shipped to his own 'English Village' at Greenfield, Massachusetts, in 1930. The cottage, which weighed just over four hundred and seventy-five tons, travelled in sixty-nine different wagons, at a cost of over £50,000. (Today's equivalent would be approximately £350,000.) Nothing was forgotten—the cottage, the dovecot, flowers, turf, well, pond, sheep, wall ... all except the garden gate. This had to be sent over later, on its own, at a cost of £440.

The Crab Cult

In the western part of New York State, America, there is a small and strange community of crab-toed people. Their peculiar affliction has puzzled doctors and scientists. The hands and feet of these people resemble the claws of a crab or a lobster. Here is part of a report by the Supervisor of the City College of New York, in April, 1976:

"The City College of New York sent a field-worker into the community where this strange progeny existed. The descriptive matter showed that there had been two hundred and eighty-four cases of crab-toes—most of whom were social outcasts in the community, such as thieves, alcoholics, etc. Although the intelligence of these people was very low, they were able to become successful workers. They did not seem especially sensitive about their peculiar condition . . .'

crab toe good for pinching things

Moon Madness

Eight years after man had first landed on the moon in 1969, a public opinion poll was taken in six villages in the heart of Morocco. Sixty per-cent of the villagers had never heard of the landings. Of the forty per-cent that had heard, over half thought that the reports had been a hoax. Several young men and women had seen the moon-walks on television or movie newsreels, but had dismissed them as "just Hollywood fakes". When asked, "Do you believe that man has been to the moon?" ninety per-cent of the villagers stared for a moment at the interviewers, and then doubled up in gales of helpless laughter.

Who's Chicken?

Over the course of several weeks in 1971, about nine hundred people in the neighbouring villages of Mbale and Kigezi, Uganda, were seized by a mad compulsion to run wildly through the streets, clutching chickens and screaming until they collapsed from exhaustion. Local natives attributed the mania to the will of departed village chieftains. However, scientists and psychologists diagnosed it as a case of mass hysteria, comparable to a laughing epidemic which had overrun the town of Bukoba, Tanganyika, the previous year.

One of the earliest recorded cases of mass hysteria was that of the "biting nuns". At a convent in Germany in the fifteenth century, several nuns mysteriously began nipping at each other. Soon this "nun-biting" spread to other convents in Germany, and ultimately to convents in Holland and Italy.

Spooky Secret

Spook Hill, in Lake Wales, Florida, is an unusual name for an unusual street. Apparently, nobody has heard of the law of gravity there, for it is blithely disobeyed every day of the year, to the amusement of tourists and natives of the area. When the handbrake is released, a car parked in neutral will roll mysteriously uphill, as will tennis balls, ball-bearings, and Florida grapefruit dropped experimentally on the ground. Even water flows uphill on Spook Hill.

"We've had all kinds of people here trying to work it out," says the mayor of Lake Wales, Carl Chesham. "Engineers and scientists come out with tripods and levels measuring the slope of the ground and go away shaking their heads. It's an optical illusion, of course, but how it works I'll never tell. I'm not going to be the one to destroy the mystery of Spook Hill."

Treasure Chest

When the infamous King Farouk of Egypt was deposed in 1952, he fled the royal palace in Cairo, leaving behind him the following strange collection of personal effects: twenty-five pocket geiger-counters, each inscribed "Measure nuclear energy yourself", a collection of fifteen thousand comics, sixteen bedside telephones, sixty walking sticks, two thousand monogrammed ties, a hundred pairs of powerful binoculars, twenty-seven cars, all of different makes but each one gold-plated, and a hundred and fifty large photographs of elephants.

C

Utterly Speechless

Reb Frommer went for thirty years without speaking a single word—and this curious penance was self-imposed. It seems that Frommer, in an outburst of temper, cursed his bride over a trivial matter on their honeymoon. Shortly afterwards she met with a mysterious death, and Frommer blamed it all on his curse, and took a vow of silence.

He was a celebrated local character of Czortkow, Poland, and when he died in 1928, the newspapers of Poland and Germany carried the story of his tragic life and the vow of silence that he never broke until his dying day.

Tongue-twister

Take a deep breath and see if you can read aloud the following entry from the Canadian Health, Education and Welfare Department's "Certified Shellfish Shippers List":

"RS: Reshippers—Shippers who tranship shucked stock, or shell stock from certified shellfish shippers. (Reshippers are not authorised to shuck or repack shellfish.) RP: Repackers—Shippers, other than the original shucker, who pack shucked shellfish . . . A repacker may shuck shellfish or act as a shell-stock shipper . . ."

Instant Barbecue

A passenger train in Cordoba, Argentina, was derailed in 1971 when it struck and killed a cow that was lazing about on the track. Nobody was injured (apart from the cow), but the appetites of the seven hundred passengers were apparently whetted by the accident. While waiting for a repair crew to arrive and set the train on its way again, the passengers dug a barbecue pit, roasted the cow over a large fire, and devoured it with gusto. (What the farmer who owned the cow thought of all this isn't recorded.)

P.S. I Love You

In 1968, an Austrian anthropologist named Hans Weizl lived for some months among the natives of northern Siberia. Throughout his stay he was constantly pestered by giggling young teenage girls, who would appear at his door and pelt him with handfuls of lice and slugs, day and night. After a while, Weizl learned that among the northern Siberians lice and slug-throwing was the traditional manner for a woman to express her love for a man, and indicate that she was available for marriage. (It makes you wonder what on earth they throw if they don't like you.)

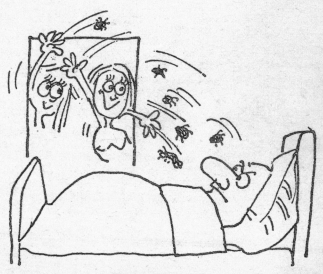

Monkey Business

Ever since the price of oil went sky-high in the 1970s, tiny Middle Eastern sheikdoms and sultanates such as Qatar and Abu Dhabi have come into more money than they know what to do with. Sheik Zaid of Abu Dhabi recently built a zoo at the Bulrami Oasis, located in the middle of the Arabian desert a hundred miles from the nearest town. Run by German-trained zoologists, the large zoo is stocked with a hundred and fifty animals and an elaborate aquarium. Water is brought in from the Persian Gulf. Queues to get into the zoo are not long, needless to say—in fact nobody goes there at all. Foreign journalists are mystified by the sheik's zeal in building a zoo in such an isolated location that nobody visits it. A spokesman for the leader said that the zoo had "improved the quality of life for his subjects."

Snow Business

On Christmas Eve, 1969, snow began falling over a seven thousand square-mile area of south-eastern Sweden. That would hardly be a remarkable occurrence, but this snow was an unusual colour—pitch black. By the morning of December 26th, several inches of black snow had entirely covered the previous deep white base. When deer walked through the dark drifts they left white footprints behind them. The Centre For Short-Lived Phenomena, Stockholm, noted that the snow was "oily and slick, and resisted removal even with detergents". The cause of the dark snowfall was never determined, although a chemical analysis did turn up traces of DDT and PCB insecticides in the black snowflakes.

Tall Story

When the American Army Corps of Engineers took over construction of the Washington Monument in 1880, they were faced with a seemingly insoluble problem: since there had been no work done on the project in twenty-five years, the ropes and scaffolding leading to the top of the monument had rotted with age. If additional bricks and mortar were to be hauled to the top, the ropes would have to be replaced, but nobody had any idea how to get the ropes to the top. The whole project seemed stymied before it had begun.

Then some bright spark had a brainstorm. Inside the hundred and fifty-six foot-high hollow shaft, a wire was tied to the leg of a pigeon. A gun was fired, and the frightened bird flew skyward, where it was killed with a blast from a second gun. The pigeon fell to the ground, still tied to the wire, which the engineers then used to haul up heavier cables and, ultimately, the scaffolding needed to complete the job.

Chomp! Chomp!

A prisoner in a German gaol literally chewed his way to freedom in 1907. The prisoner was Hans Schaarschmidt, who was serving a six-year sentence for robbery. The prison was a decaying fortress in Gera, whose windows were barred with pairs of crossed heavy wooden beams. Each day Schaarschmidt chewed away as much as his teeth could stand, then, to avoid suspicion, he filled in the holes in the beams with a rubbery paste made from the bread he was fed. After three months, Schaarschmidt was able to remove the bread putty and squeeze through to freedom.

Look Mum — No Bridge!

In Argentina in 1966, a band of thieves dismantled and absconded with a large iron bridge spanning the River Rio Panara. The nocturnal theft was discovered the following morning when rush-hour traffic became uncustomarily congested on the various approaches to the bridge. Argentinian police were able to trace the bridge to a local scrap-metal dealer who had purchased it from the thieves. But the criminals were never caught.

Tasteful Trip

If you're crazy about waste-disposal (and everybody ought to have a hobby), you will find a guided tour of the Paris sewers utterly fascinating. Parisians are justifiably proud of having the finest system in the world. The vast maze of pipes, sumps and subterranean tunnels is considered one of the great achievements of civil engineering. But that doesn't necessarily make it a pleasant place to visit, nor would you want to live there. This famous underground excursion (the tour costs the equivalent of £1 and lasts for three hours) will be hard to forget—the echoes are ghostly, and the weird sights, sounds and smells will linger with you for ages.

The French have the finest sewers in the world...

The Visible Man

In the sixteenth century, a man in Yu t'ien, China, named Hsieh Hsuan, was born with transparent flesh. The veins, bones and organs of his body were clearly visible. Hsieh was a great scholar and attained the Chu Jen Degree, a high honour. He began an official career, but became implicated in a bribery case and was sentenced to death. He continued his studies in prison, and even when he was led out to be executed he was calmly reading a book on astrology. At the very last minute he was reprieved, and later canonised. In 1572 his tablet of canonisation was placed in the Confucian Temple, where it still remains.

Having a Canniball

During the Vietnamese war of 1972, a government paymaster made the mistake of dropping in empty-handed on a unit of battle-weary Cambodian soldiers, encamped near Pnom Penh, who hadn't been paid for months. When the soldiers' demand for their back wages was rebuffed, they shot the paymaster and ate him.

In fact, Cambodian warriors have for years considered the flesh of their adversaries tasty fare, and an enemy's internal organs—the liver, in particular—are considered a great source of strength and fighting prowess. The soldiers who feasted on fillet of paymaster told reporters afterwards that while fighting at Kompong Seila, eighty miles south-west of the Cambodian capital, they had hungrily devoured the bodies of several Khmer Rouge rebels slain in battle.

Old Romeo

Following a long bout of pneumonia, thirty-five-year-old Francois de Civille of Milan was declared dead in October, 1562. Accordingly he was buried. Six hours later—on some strange intuition of his brother—he was disinterred, and revived. De Civille lived seventy more years—dying at the old age of a hundred and five from bronchitis, contracted "serenading the lady of his heart all night long". This time they laid him to rest for ever.

Bright Ideas Department

Karl Frederick Gauss, one of the most inventive mathematicians of all time, proposed that hundreds of square miles in the Siberian steppes be planted with seventeen-mile-long lines of pine trees, symbolically representing the Pythagorean theorem. The pattern, Gauss believed, would communicate to observers on other planets the fact that the earth was inhabited by creatures intelligent enough to know geometry—and therefore worthy of a visit.

But what should mankind's reaction be when outer-space beings land on Earth and make themselves known? At a meeting of the International Astronomical Union in London, in 1975, the distinguished astronomer Dr Hewish recommended that on that fateful day, "We should call a special meeting of the Royal Society and inform all the politicians. Then the world would be told and a suitable reply to the aliens would be drafted."

Cash For Your Corpse

Lars Venson, a Swedish sailor out of a job and in need of money in 1840, sold his body to the Royal Swedish Institute of Anatomy for £12. The Institute had the right to claim his body on his death and use it how they liked in the dissection laboratories. However, Lars was blessed with fortune, and twenty years later he had enough money to buy back the rights to his corpse from the Institute. But the Institute refused to co-operate, so Lars took his case to court—where he lost. Worst of all, he had to re-imburse the Institute for two teeth that he'd had extracted without their permission.

In any event, Lars might have done a bit better had he lived today. For in 1974 the total market value of a human body, including fat, milk, blood, bones, pimples, hair, muscle-tissue, ash, assorted fluids, etc, was approximately £116.

Good Grub

The Chinese emperor, Ch'eng Tung, ordered his chief minister, I Yin, to prepare an inventory of the most tasty foods available in all the world. I Yin's selections, compiled in the year 1500 BC, included the following: the lips from the orang-outan ape. The tails of young swallows. The knees of the elephant. The tail of the yak. The blue mushrooms from the Yang-hua valley. Sardines from the Eastern sea. Duckweed from rivers sheltered by yew trees. Sauce made from sturgeon, leeks, cinnamon and lichens.

Nasal Nightmare

While studying at the University of Rostock, the Danish astronomer Tycho Brahe was insulted by a fellow student, and promptly challenged him to a duel. In the following contest, Brahe's nose was sliced off with a sword. Noseless, he commissioned a jeweller to make him a brilliant new nose out of gold and silver, which he wore for the rest of his life. The man with the golden nose is best remembered for his precise observations of the heavens, which paved the way for the discoveries of Kepler and Newton. The largest crater on the moon is named in Tycho's honour.

Pardon Me!

In the small town of Raleigh, Mississippi, a National Spitting Contest is held every year. The local politicians come along to the event to shake hands, and the champion spitters come along to do what comes naturally. In 1976, a man named Don Snyder set a new spitting record by propelling a portion of spit—tobacco-flavoured—the distance of thirty-one feet, one inch. To prepare for the finals, Snyder spat conscientiously every day for two months beforehand. He claims that he owed his spitting prowess to his mother, who taught him how to chew and spit, and in her prime "could hit the fireplace from any spot in the room and never get a mark upon the floor."

Beware the Widow

In 1974, six successive husbands of the same Polynesian woman all died of anaemia less than a month after their wedding days. The unlucky bride, Sai Kulkenkos, consulted a witch doctor for an explanation. The witch doctor attributed the deaths to the spirit of a vampire that had inhabited Sai's body, and sucked her husbands' blood from their bodies. (So far there have been no reports of Sai receiving a seventh proposal of marriage.)

HISTORY BOOK. Acts of Utter Lunacy etc by. A.TWIT.

Contemporary Half-Wits

CHAPTER FIVE

Historical Hysteria

Wouldn't it have been fun to have Sir Francis Drake's ship, the *Golden Hind*, balanced on top of St Paul's Cathedral? Alas, it never happened, though it nearly came to be, as you'll find out in this chapter, which is sub-titled "Acts of Utter Lunacy and Stupidity Through the Ages, as Witnessed by Contemporary Half-Wits". Which is quite a long sub-title, but then, history is pretty long, too. Don't run away though; this isn't the kind of history you normally have to suffer at school. Here you'll be entertained with tales of sailors swigging rum, railway trains colliding, the world being sold, and men breaking into houses to dig up floors!

Queenly Prices

An extract from Queen Victoria's household accounts for the year 1857 reads thus:

	(Per Annum)		
Poet Laureate:	£72	0s	0d
Rat Catcher:	£88	5s	0d
Dentist:	£100	0s	0d
Chimney Sweep:	£125	17s	6d
Stableman:	£62	1s	0d
Pantry Maid:	£21	0s	0d
Veterinary Surgeon:	£43	15s	0d
Croquet Mallets:	£1	4s	6d

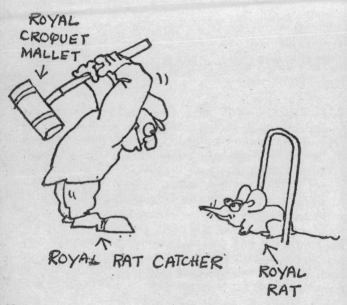

ROYAL CROQUET MALLET

ROYAL RAT CATCHER

ROYAL RAT

Roasted Royalty

When King George IV was crowned in July, 1821, he was so afraid of trouble at his coronation that he engaged a gang of prize-fighters to act as pages to carry his train. The train was over thirty-two feet long. King George wished the public to see his ornate costume, and was heard to direct his pages: "Hold it wider, ye ignorant scum!" When the King withdrew temporarily to change, all the pugilistic "pages" were seen scurrying about, eating and drinking and fighting with people. One of them wrapped a piece of chicken in a length of the red train and tossed it to his sweetheart. The heat was so intense inside Westminster Abbey that the King used thirty-five handkerchiefs during the crowning ceremony.

Naval Treaties

As early as 1590, the Royal Navy used to issue each sailor with a ration of one gallon of strong beer every day. By the eighteenth century, as an alternative to the beer ration, a sailor could either have a pint of wine or half a pint of rum. The rum ration was reduced to a quarter-pint in 1880, reduced further to a small tot in 1907, and finally abolished in 1970. Many people wonder why the traditional navy drink of rum-and-water is known as "grog". This name lives on in memory of a certain Admiral Vernon—who first introduced the mixture—because of his penchant for wearing "grogram", a material made out of mohair and silk.

ORIGIN
OF THE
WORD
GROGGY"

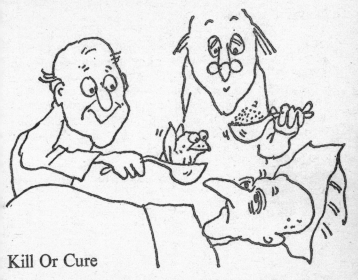

Kill Or Cure

In February, 1685, King Charles II died of a stroke—or so say his official biographers. In truth, it was probably the treatment for the stroke that did him in. On the morning of the stroke, twelve physicians were summoned to the royal chambers, and they immediately started to purge all the poisons from the king's body. First they relieved him of a quart of blood, then shaved his scalp and singed it with red-hot irons. Then they filled his nose with sneezing powder and blanketed him with hot plasters, which they then tore off. The treatment produced no results, and Charles sank quickly. Frantically, the doctors bombed the monarch with more bleedings, purgatives, and fed him with mysterious potions learnt from ancient books—powdered horse's skull, pearls dissolved in ammonia, the skin of frogs, rook's feathers soaked in ass's milk... but nothing worked. On the fifth day, after quietly apologising for taking so long to die, Charles breathed his last—perhaps with some relief.

AH-KWEI LIVED IN THE GOLDEN AGE OF HAPPINESS

Relatively Speaking

Ah-Kwei, of Kansu, China, was a great-great-great-great-great-great-great-great-grandfather! He lived to see his descendants down to the tenth generation. He was presented to the son of the son of the son of the son of the son of the son of the son of the son of the son of *his* son! Ah-Kwei lived in the Golden Age of Happiness. And when the Emperor of China was searching for the happiest man in his empire, the Kansu patriarch was brought before him.

In 1790, Ah-Kwei had a hundred and thirty-five living great-great-great-great-great-great-great-great grandchildren. One shudders at the thought of his Christmas present bill!

As You'd Like to Find It . . .

Incredible as it seems, thirty centuries of scientific progress have not improved the ring of dirt left behind in the bath. In 1973, Israeli archeologists unearthed a three thousand year-old bathtub from the ancient Mycenaean palace at Pylos in Greece. When they trained infra-red rays on the relic they found a three thousand year-old ring of dirt as well. Invisible to the naked eye, the ring consisted of decomposed body oils, dead bacteria, and assorted organic detritus.

Vile Victuals

The Compte de Volney, a French nobleman visiting England for the first time in 1864, wrote back home in disgust: "If a prize were devised for a regimen most calculated to injure the stomach, the teeth, and the health in general, no better could be invented than that of the English. In the mornings at breakfast they indulge in a quart of hot water, slightly impregnated with tea so it tastes like hot water. Then they swallow, almost without chewing, half-baked toast soaked in butter, cheese of the fattest kind, slices of beef or ham, etc. At dinner, they have nasty boiled pastes under the name of puddings, salt meat, oysters, with their vegetables swimming in hog's lard. Supper again passes in heaping one indigestion on another, and to give tone to the poor, wearied stomach, they drink Madeira, rum, French brandy and gin by the pint."

Floating Fools

It was the policy of many towns in sixteenth century Germany to gather together the insane and imprison them on large river-boats. These floating lunatic asylums were known as "Narrenschiffs", or "ships of fools". The "Narrenschiffs" served as a dual purpose: to hand a madman over to a sailor was to be permanently certain that he would not prowl about the cities terrifying people and, secondly, it was thought at the time that the insane had literally lost their souls, and thus the ships of fools were pilgrimage boats carrying "cargoes of madmen in search of their reason". Some went down the Rhineland rivers toward Belgium and Ghent, some sailed up the Rhine toward the Jura and Bensancon. Some just sailed away and were never seen again.

Marriage Aids

In 1770, a Bill was introduced in Parliament, "denouncing women who wrongly seduce men into marriage by the use of costly scents, paints, cosmetic washes, artificial limbs, false hair, false teeth, iron stays and corsets, hoops, high-heeled shoes, and bolstered bosoms and hips."

If a woman was convicted of capturing a husband by any of these means, the marriage would be declared null and void. The Bill never did become law—fortunately for the state of matrimony. For there cannot have been a single wife, dead or alive, who did not resort to at least one of the crimes listed!

Faulty Tower

The tower of the parish church at Farnborough, Kent, is noticeably squat and low—only thirty-five feet high. There is, of course, a good reason for this. The previous towers were: blown down in 1639; destroyed by fire in 1688; blown down in 1724; blown down in 1838.

The fifth, and present tower, was badly damaged by fire in 1949, but still stands.

Bang! Marks The Spot

The "Monument" in London, the two hundred and two feet high column by the River Thames, was erected in 1676 to commemorate the Great Fire of London, at a cost of £2,000. Seventeen workers lost their lives in the construction of it. The strange thing about the Monument is that if it were to fall (or be lowered) due east, its top would rest on the exact spot where the Great Fire of London started, in Pudding Lane.

Drunken Davy

For most of his term as congressman from Tennessee during the 1830s, the legendary Davy Crockett dozed quietly in his chair in Congress and kept very quiet. But there was one issue he felt so passionately about that he was compelled to speak out—the prohibition of whisky sales inside the Capitol building. In a memorable speech, Davy Crockett declared that whisky in Congress should not only be legal but should be provided free. "Congress allows lemonade to members, and it is charged under the heading of stationery," Davy declared. "I move that whisky be allowed under the heading of necessary fuel."

Cheap Cabinets

When Ramsay Macdonald became Prime Minister in 1924, and moved into No. 10 Downing Street, he found the house practically bare of furniture except for a few chairs and some threadbare curtains. Luckily, an aunt of his went to the sales, and managed to furnish the entire place with new curtains, wallpaper and furniture at bargain prices—including a double bed for £2, a wardrobe for £1, fifty gallons of paint for £3, a refectory table for £4, and a thirty-four piece dinner-service for only ten shillings.

World For Sale

After the death of Pertinax, the Roman world was offered for sale by the all-powerful Praetorian Guard. Didius Salvius Julianus Marcus, a wealthy Roman merchant, outbid all others, and the world was knocked down to him after he had paid the equivalent in gold of £2,500,000 in 193 A.D. The Roman Senate took the oath of loyalty to him.

When the Roman Legions stationed in Britain learned of the disgraceful deal, they rose in indignation. Under the leadership of General Septimus Severus, they hurried to Rome, where Didius was seized, deposed and beheaded, just a month after he'd purchased the world. Septimus thereupon became the Emperor of Rome.

Saltpetre Scoundrels

By an Act of Parliament in 1630, "Saltpetre Men" were allowed to dig anywhere—even under people's floors and in their walls—for the saltpetre necessary for making gunpowder. The only places where they weren't allowed were "private bedrooms or rooms where the newly-dead lay".

One irate grocer from Croydon, Surrey, complained to Parliament that the dreaded Saltpetre Men were ruining his business "by digging up the cellars of my shop, knocking down the walls and burying my stock, and knocking over customers in pursuit of their vile trade!"

Don't Panic!

A British telegraph message received in London from Waterloo on June 19th, 1815, started: "WELLINGTON DEFEATED ..." Immediately Stock Exchange prices tumbled to a new low and the city flew into a terrible panic. In the confusion, several rich merchant bankers believed they had lost their fortunes and committed suicide. But the banking firm of Rothschilds bought all the shares they could lay their hands on, and at incredibly cheap prices. This was the start of their immense family fortune. For their own carrier pigeon had beaten the new and slow optical telegraph system and relayed the whole message: "WELLINGTON DEFEATED THE FRENCH AT WATERLOO."

Ba-ba Black Bank

In the early part of the nineteenth century a special bank operated in Aberystwyth in South Wales called "The Bank of Black Sheep". This curious bank was formed in 1810 in an effort to foil highway robbers. The problem was that Welsh farmers, having driven their sheep to market, often had trouble getting home with their money intact. So, to avoid carrying hard cash with them, they formed their own bank. It issued notes ranging in value from £1 to £10. The novel part about the notes was that they were engraved with a large black sheep—the number of sheep in the engraving counting the value in pounds. A lamb counted for ten shillings (50p). The idea didn't seem to catch on, for "The Bank of Black Sheep" went bust after only four years.

Setting an Example

At the opening of the new city workhouse in Southampton in 1832, the lecture given to the assembled paupers was an hour and a half's talk on "Thrift". The dinner given for the V.I.P.'s attending the workhouse opening included the following: lobster, roast chicken, ham, veal patties, tongue, wine jellies, cherry tarts, savoy cakes, and eleven different kinds of wine. For the inmates, however, the fare was a little more restricted: bread and lard, bread and margarine, unsweetened cocoa.

Monumental Disaster

Lord Nelson was responsible for a common fallacy about many sculptors—that, on discovering some defect or inaccuracy in their statues, they promptly committed suicide from shame and humiliation. The Britannia memorial to Lord Nelson at Great Yarmouth faces inland. Many people think it should be facing the sea, and there is a local legend that the architect, on realising the "mistake", hurled himself from the top and was no more. However, the hundred and forty-four feet high monument was intentionally placed to face inland towards Burnham Thorpe, Nelson's birthplace. The suicide legend probably arose after Thomas Sutton, the superintendent of works, collapsed and fell to his death when climbing the two hundred and seventeen steps of the monument after its completion in June, 1819.

Innocent Criminal

Viscount Castlereagh, one of the keenest intellects and greatest statesmen of the Napoleonic period, started acting rather strangely at the age of forty-seven, in 1815. On one occasion he knelt before King George IV and confessed to all manner of crimes, including treason, and the murder of Lord Palmerston—who was in the room at the time! He complained to the Speaker of the House of Commons that the House was empty when it was nearly full, and he would deny the existence of a piece of paper that he held in his hand. It seemed that years of hard work and worry had affected his brain. King George sent his own doctor to look after Castlereagh at his house in North Cray, Kent. His razors and guns were removed, but nonetheless he committed suicide by cutting his throat with a pair of nail scissors in 1822.

Time, Gentlemen, Please

The clock on Big Ben stopped on January 14th 1955—the first time for over a hundred years. A large lump of snow had frozen under the minute hand and had stopped the clock at 3.25 a.m. Incidentally, you cannot see Big Ben from the street. For Big Ben is the bell inside the tower, named in memory of twenty-five-stone Benjamin Hall, an eighteenth century politician.

D

Eureka Streaker!

The word "Eureka" (which is Greek for "I've found it!") became famous when used by the mathematician Archimedes on discovering the principle that bodies can be weighed according to their displacement of water. The tradition is that Archimedes made his dramatic discovery when he stepped into his bath one day and observed the water overflowing. He immediately bolted out into the street, crying "Eureka! Eureka!" Thus Archimedes not only discovered the important principle—he also inadvertently invented streaking.

Well-protected Mail

In October, 1770, newly-designed mail-carts, constructed of cast-iron, carried the Northern Mail. But upon arrival at Enfield, Middlesex, the Postmaster could not find a way to open the mail-carts. He and his assistants struggled for two days without any success. In the end they had to send for the maker, who lived in Liverpool, to instruct the postal workers how to open the mail-carts.

Ship Ahoy!

When Sir Francis Drake's famous ship, the *Golden Hind*—in which he had sailed around the world—arrived back in London in 1580, the nation went wild. It was seriously suggested that the ship should be set on top of the spire of St Paul's Cathedral (estimates for the task came to £10,000). Another scheme was that the *Golden Hind* be moored on the lawns of Buckingham Palace, or even housed inside the palace itself. However, these plans came to nought. The *Golden Hind* was left moored in the Thames at Deptford in London. Within two years it had been pulled to pieces by souvenir-hunters, and not a single splinter of it was left.

Phoney Singer

At the grand opening ceremony of the Crystal Palace in 1851, among the foreign ambassadors was a Chinaman with the rather improbable name of He Sing Well. He was assumed to be representing his country, was duly announced and took part in the opening performances. Later he was discovered to be the owner of a small Chinese laundry establishment in Soho.

Not Amused

During her life, Queen Victoria would never allow the royal train to exceed 30 mph. (Once, when travelling from London to Brighton, the train reached the speed of 40 mph. When she found out, the Queen had the driver whipped and sacked from his job.) However, when, in 1901, Queen Victoria's body was brought from the Isle of Wight to Windsor, the train from Southampton started ten minutes late. The train touched 95 mph on occasion, and rocked violently on some of the curves.

Perfect Prediction

The American writer Mark Twain (real name Samuel Leghorn Clemens) was born in 1834, the time when Halley's Comet had just been sighted and was front-page news all over the world. Later, Twain commented in an article: "I came in with the Comet, and I expect to go out with it." Mark Twain died in 1910, just a few days before the re-appearance of the Comet.

CHAPTER SIX

Art Attacks

Ever since the first caveman painted a picture of his local football team on a cave wall, mankind has been seized with the urge to create. Usually he creates an awful mess, but no matter. For here is a small but select catalogue of some of the most awful artistic disasters known to civilised man—a kind of cultural rubbish bin. Read all about the man with the twenty-one-feet-high double bass, and the weird attempts at poetry by a computer—not to mention the invention of the mobile cinema ...

Cupid's Corner

The statue of Eros in London's Piccadilly Circus has been the cause of wonderment for many years. Just why was a Greek god of fertility chosen as the memorial for an English philanthropist? For the popular statue is in memory of Lord Shaftesbury, and was sculpted by a certain Sir Alfred Gilbert. When Eros was unveiled in 1893 it didn't have a name. But Sir Alfred was reported as saying to a friend: "I think it looks rather like Eros, don't you?" And thus it has remained, quite unofficially.

Penny Poems

They used to say that if you locked a dozen chimpanzees in a room equipped with typewriters for a thousand years, one of them would eventually type out the works of Shakespeare. Today the process has been refined and accelerated through the use of high-speed computers. An operator can feed a basic vocabulary into a machine's memory, programme it, and, *voila!*—instant poetry. Here are a few early attempts at computer verses:

> Under a lamp the nude is vain,
> Cabbage is often blind.
> Life reached through empty faces,
> Space flowed over the beetroot.

A computer at Cambridge Language Research Institute was programmed to compose a love poem. The result:

> All black white in the buds,
> I flash snowballs in the spring,
> Bang the sun has gone away.

Collected Works of Nixon, Keats and Shelley

In the wake of America's Watergate scandals in 1976, a small cassette company in Paris named Peerless Enterprises brought out a nifty little novelty package—a recording of President Nixon's resignation speech accompanied by printed transcripts in French and English. But the address was short and only lasted seven minutes. So the tape was padded out with poems by Keats, Shelley, Wordsworth and Rimbaud.

Up, Up and Away

In 1972, jazz composer Roger Kellaway composed a modern ballet, rather mysteriously called "P.A.M.T.G.G." The work was premiered at New York's Lincoln Centre, featuring the stars of the New York City Ballet. As soon as the audience (who were wondering what the initials of the ballet's title stood for) heard the opening bars, they got the joke. The basic theme for the twenty-five minute score was borrowed from a television commericial, "Pan-Am Makes The Going Great". The exuberant choreography included impressions of aeroplane take-offs, landings, and the inevitable scramble by passengers for their luggage.

Dud Van Dyck

In the Municipal Art Museum in Danzig, Poland, there hung two paintings by famous artists—one by Breughel the Elder, and one by Van Dyck. Nobody noticed anything odd about them until 1972, when the Breughel mysteriously fell off the wall one day. It turned out not to be the original, but a reproduction cut out of a magazine. The Van Dyck was similarly faked. Nobody knows for certain when the originals (worth up to half a million pounds) were stolen, though scientific examination of the magazine cuttings and the picture frames indicate that it was probably about ten years before the discovery of the theft was noticed.

A Really High Note

Michaele Jullien, an eccentric composer and conductor from Paris, introduced a twenty-one-feet-tall High Octo Basso (a kind of king-sized double-bass) into his orchestra during the summer season at Drury Lane in 1972. The booming sounds of the Octo Basso drowned out all the other instruments, and Jullien admitted that he'd made a mistake in including such an absurd instrument. "Perhaps my new drum set will be more successful," he said, producing a bass drum that measured eighteen feet across. Any replies he had to this suggestion were not recorded.

Terse Verse

One of the shortest poems in the world must be:

> Hired.
> Tired?
> Fired!

There is one, however, which is even shorter. Anonymously written, like the first, it is called "Lines Written On The Great Antiquity Of Microbes":

> Adam
> Had 'em.

Cash For Your Trash

Since 1974, the earnings of hack writers and purveyors of other rubbish in its various forms have been subjected to a special "Trash Tax" in Hungary. The tax is levied by the Minister of Culture, and put in a special "Culture Fund" used to endow nobler artistic endeavours.

Of course, the difference between art and trash is hard to tell. But it's something that the Budapest culture vultures know. Trash, by their definition, is anything that panders to popular tastes. Sentimental paintings of children, mystery novels by best-selling authors, plastic flowers, ugly furniture, pop music, television serials—all of these are labelled trash, and their producers are taxed heavily for them.

Dog Eat Dog

At an open-air concert in Juarezeiro do Norte, Brazil, in the summer of 1973, a singer named Waldick Sorano was giving a performance of a humorous song called "I Am Not A Dog". Suddenly, halfway through the song, a dog trotted on stage, wearing a large sign that read "I Am Not Waldick Sorano". Infuriated by the practical joke, Sorano stopped singing, chased the dog offstage and started insulting the audience, who were in fits of laughter. The audience retaliated by slinging rotten peaches and tomatoes at him. A free-for-all fight ensued, and Sorano was forced offstage and chased all the way back to his hotel room.

The Film Standing on Platform Seven . . .

Beginning on May 1st, 1935, the 10.10 train from Kings Cross, London, was fitted with a special coach for the showing of new films. Known as the "Cinema Special", the coach was equipped with a five-feet by four-feet screen, and seating for fifty-two passengers. Admission to the (literally) moving pictures was a shilling (5p). When the train returned to London is the afternoon a different film was shown. In 1936, similar services were introduced on the London to Edinburgh line, and a few others. But then came the war and, sadly, the notion of seeing a movie in movement was cast aside in favour of faster trains.

CHAPTER SEVEN

Murder and Other Silly Sports

Can you see the connection between a public execution and an underwater golf tournament? Or the similarity between a cricket match and the murder of a Prime Minister? Well, they all provide entertainment for the masses and are quite cheap to run. Thus we arrive at Wit's End, the final chapter of this book. Crime and sport have always conspired to produce deeds of great heroism—but you won't find any of them here. Instead, you'll find ghosts and ghouls lurking, killers creeping, thieves thinking, and bad-losers booing. All the dregs of humanity are here, so step right up and see the fun of the foul. (You have nothing to lose but your sanity).

Cool Corpses

Until the late 1880s there were no mortuaries in Britain to store the recently dead. Corpses used to be taken into public houses—usually the cellars—to await inquest and burial. But one publican at Chislehurst, Kent, on a hot summer's day in 1887, found that a dead body delivered to him for storage was "a little too high". So he refused to have it on his premises. As a result of this there was a large-scale governmental enquiry, and shortly afterwards the first mortuaries came into being.

Deadly Dreams

Spencer Percival was the only British Prime Minister to be murdered. He was shot dead in the lobby of the House of Commons on May 11th, 1921, by John Bellingham, a merchant who believed that his bankruptcy was the direct result of the government's politics.

This crime was allegedly foreseen by a certain John Williams of Redruth, in Cornwall, in three successive dreams just before the murder. In each dream he was in the House of Commons and "saw a person in a snuff-coloured coat draw a gun and shoot a small man in a blue suit and a white waistcoat." This is exactly how the murder happened and, two days before the incident, Williams wrote to Percival warning him. John Bellingham was adjudged to be insane, but was nonetheless hanged.

Changing Charges

At the quarterly Littlehampton Assizes in March, 1817, the jury found James Tyson, a Sussex labourer, guilty of stealing a pair of corduroy breeches and a cotton shirt. According to the laws of the day, the penalty for Tyson's crime was hanging. Appalled at this, the jury asked permission for the charge to be changed from theft to something a little less lethal. Sarcastically, the judge said, "Yes—you can change it to manslaughter if you like!" This they did—and James Tyson pleaded guilty to murdering a stranger whose body had disappeared, was fined one shilling and fourpence ... and was promptly released!

The Berkeley Square Beast

In 1870, a shapeless horror, seen only at night, began to terrorise people at No. 50 Berkeley Square, in London's Mayfair. Among the victims the horror claimed were a young sailor who threw himself from a top window and was found dead, a housemaid who died from fright, a soldier who was found dead without a mark on his body, and an old woman discovered in a cupboard who had been dead for weeks. There were countless cases of hysteria from the various occupants over the years. In 1906 the owners offered the property rent-free to anybody who would take it, but it remained empty for over twenty years. Nowadays, the shapeless horror seems to have moved on, and a publishing firm occupies the once dreaded No. 50 Berkeley Square.

Stiff Sentence

Sir Charles Mompesson, found guilty in 1632 of blackmail, arson, cruelty and threatening tradesmen, was sentenced to the following: to lose his knighthood, pay a £10,000 fine, suffer a hundred strokes of the whip, forfeit his property and valuables, walk down the Strand with his face to a horse's tail, held forever to be an infamous rogue—and then to be imprisoned for life. However, through an underground system of bribery and corruption, Sir Charles was pardoned and died peacefully in 1671 on his vast country estate in Shropshire.

Pewter Pilferer

In 1614, a certain William Fielde (alias Bold-faced Will) was charged and found guilty of stealing the following: "seven pewter platters, six pewter pottle pots, three pewter mugs, two pewter posset pots, a pewter basin, a pewter medal—and a cloak worth four shillings and sixpence."

Stamp Out Poverty!

Adolf Hitler was quite poor when he came to power as leader of the Nazi party. But a clever idea of Martin Bormann's soon made the Fuehrer extremely rich. Hitler, his personal photographer, and Bormann decided that Hitler had rights to the reproduction of his picture on postage stamps, and was therefore entitled to payment... Since the Fuehrer's head appeared on all stamps—those issued between 1933 and 1945—millions of pounds flowed into Hitler's bank account.

What's Life?

The Californian Herald, in August 1926, carried the following strange piece of news: "Bill Warner has just returned from the Death Valley country. Bill worked for six years on the graveyard shift for the Corpse Mining Company in the Coffin Mine, located in Dead Man's Canyon in Funeral Range at the end of Death Valley. Bill is leaving next week for a prospecting trip to the Devil's Playground in Hell's Half-Acre."

Berlin Butchery

Meat was extremely scarce and expensive in Berlin in the 1920s. But an enterprising butcher named Karl Denke was able to sell high-quality smoked pork at incredibly low prices. Denke's many customers, though baffled by his modest rates, asked no questions.

However, had they chewed their food more reflectively, they would have tasted something decidedly un-porklike. When Denke became involved in a loud argument with a neighbour, local police came around to check. While they were there they searched his premises ... They uncovered several barrels of freshly-smoked human flesh, along with boxfuls of bones and a healthy supply of human lard—all distilled from the carcasses of Denke's fifty-two murder victims. They also discovered a ledger book, with the date of each killing, and the weight of the victim, recorded in the butcher's neat writing.

116

Fore!

In 1912, a woman golfer at Shawnee, Pennsylvania, misjudged her shot and sliced her ball into the Delaware River. Her husband rowed her after it while she took shot after shot, sending up great fountains of water, trying to reach it. Eventually, after struggling for an hour, she landed the ball one and half miles away, and then had to play it all the way back to the green. Her total for this hole (the sixteenth) was a record-breaking hundred and fifty-six strokes. Shortly after this she gave up golf for horse riding.

Sporting Spaceman

Astronaut Alan Shepard, who took a six-iron golf club and a packet of balls on board his Apollo XIV spacecraft, became the first golfer on the moon, in February, 1971. Despite a busy work schedule and his cumbersome space-suit, Shepard was able to get in some practice during an extra-vehicular walk. His worst shot in the airless, low-gravity environment travelled about four hundred yards on the fine lunar dust. "Not bad for a six-iron," Shepard remarked. As he later explained to President Nixon, "No matter how badly you hit the balls, they always go dead straight."

Fun and Games

When, after a two thousand year rest, the Olympic Games were revived in 1896, the tug-of-war, standing long jump, and one-handed weight-lifting were listed on the official programme alongside the classic events. And at the 1904 games in Madrid there were two featured events lacking somewhat in the usual Olympian dignity. The "barrel-jump" was an absurd obstacle course littered with old wine casks that athletes clambered over and leapt through. Less slapstick, but equally odd, was the half-hundredweight rock throw, won by a Canadian policeman, Etienne Desmateau, with a manly heave of thirty-four feet four inches.

Maiden Over

Until the year 1840, all cricketers used to bowl underarm. Then one day in the summer of that year, when a Somerset girl named Christine Willis was bowling to her brother, she had to bowl overarm because of the then-fashionable, wide, crinoline-type skirts. The method slowly spread, for it became obvious that one could bowl a lot faster that way. After years of disputes with umpires, overarm bowling gradually became accepted. So if it hadn't been for young Christine's skirts, underarm bowling would still be used today, even in Test Matches.

Near Miss

A coach carrying a team of seven Japanese acrobats plunged from a five hundred-feet-high cliff near Tokyo in 1955. Death seemed inevitable as the vehicle careered violently down the mountainside, overturning several times. A few hundred feet down, however, the coach's progress was stemmed for a split second when it struck a large rock. In that instant the seven men hurled themselves through open windows and landed in the branches of a tree, bruised, battered and dazed—but alive.

Double Trouble

In the twelfth round of a boxing match between two fighters named Henry Cartwright and Davy Ellis, held in Wigan, Lancashire, in June, 1912, there was a rather unusual finish to the proceedings. Both boxers knocked their opponent out simultaneously. As they lay sprawled in a heap on the canvas, the referee scratched his head, then acted quickly. Seizing the arm of the man on top, Davy Ellis, he promptly declared him the winner.

Parking Tickets

In Kelsey Park, Beckenham, Kent, you may not, according to a sign displaying ancient bye-laws, do any of the following things: play a musical instrument, shake out your mats or carpets, practice gymnastics, drive a horse-drawn bus.

Nor, if you happen to be "infested with vermin", may you "lie about by day" in the park.

Tug-of-water

There was once a somewhat curious tug-of-war between two boats. It was the result of a great controversy concerning the merits of paddle-power over propeller-power. The propeller driven ship, named *Rattler*, was attached, stern to stern, to a paddle-wheeler, the *Necto*, in the North Sea in April, 1845. The great battle commenced. Both vessels had two hundred horsepower engines, but, when working at full power, the *Rattler* towed the *Necto* backwards at a speed of two and a half knots for a distance of over five miles.

Foul Play

Alec Brooks, a table-tennis champion of the 1930s, once played a match on an ice-rink surface. He wore special shoes and a safety helmet, as did his opponent. At one point in the match Brooks slipped, fell over, grabbed at the table, and skidded with it into the side of the ice-skating rink, smashing the table to pieces. The umpire solemnly gave the point to Brooks' opponent—Brooks, he said, had touched the table.

Crazy — But True!
More Crazy — But True!

Compiled by Jonathan Clements

With drawings by Roger Smith

Flummox your Family and Flabbergast your Friends
with these two feasts of fascinating facts.

Do you know . . .
Which English duke was allergic to cabbage?
Where you may not eat snakes on Sundays?
The world's longest swearword?

Find out the answers—along with hundreds more
Staggering Snippets of Invaluable Information.

They're all quite Crazy—But True!

Armada

The Armada Book of Jokes & Riddles
The first torture-chamber to appear in paperback!

Compiled by Jonathan Clements

with drawings by Roger Smith

The 2nd Armada Book of Jokes & Riddles
The only bottle of laughing gas ever to explode into print!

Do you want to . . .
Drive your friends around the bend?
See your enemies go green and shrivel up?
Turn teachers into gibbering jelly-blobs?
Make strong men go pale at the knees?
Giggle yourself silly?
You do?

Then come on in—and laugh till your ears drop off!

Armada

The Trickster's Handbook
200 tricks, jokes and stunts to fool your friends

Peter Eldin

Instant Magic!
Astonish your friends in 200 hilarious ways.
Prove that 19 equals 20 ... tear a telephone directory
in half ... tell fortunes with a banana ... float a
sausage in mid-air ...

How's it done? Only you know, when you've got a
copy of The Trickster's Handbook. So keep it in a
secret place while you baffle your victims with
fiendish stunts and leg-pulls.

Another exciting Fun Book from Armada

Armada